THE ARTS

Written by

EMILIE DUFRESNE

Designed by

DANIELLE RIPPENGILL

BookLife
PUBLISHING

©2021
BookLife Publishing Ltd.
King's Lynn
Norfolk PE30 4LS

A catalogue record for this book is available from the British Library.

ISBN: 978-1-83927-175-5

Written by:
Emilie Dufresne

Edited by:
Madeline Tyler

Designed by:
Danielle Rippengill

Image Credits

All images are courtesy of Shutterstock.com, unless otherwise specified. With thanks to Getty Images, Thinkstock Photo and iStockphoto. Cover – cosmaa, View6424, Sundry Studio. Heading typface used throughout – cosmaa. Images used on every page – cosmaa, Sundry Studio. 14 – curiosity. 16 – Macrovector. 18 – robin.ph. 19&20 – Gaidamashchuk. 20 – robin.ph. 25 – Tatahnka. 29 – Denis Makarenko, DFree, Ovidiu Hrubaru, Phonesvanh Siharat.

CONTENTS

Words that look like **this** are explained in the glossary on page 30.

HAVING PRIDE

What Does It Mean to Have Pride?

To have pride means to feel good and worthy about who you are or what you have done. You can also feel pride for other people, and be proud of who they are and what they have done. Having pride can bring people pleasure and make them happy.

What Is Pride?

As well as being a word to describe how people feel, Pride is also a march and a celebration of people from the LGBTQIA+ community. Many towns and cities across the world hold Pride marches and celebrations. They are a time for people to celebrate who they are and remind everyone of what still needs to be achieved for those in the LGBTQIA+ community.

What Does LGBTQIA+ Mean?

The letters that make up LGBTQIA+ mean many different things about sex, sexuality and gender identity.

Sex

A person's sex is to do with their biology. It can refer to the biological sex they were assigned at birth, or it could be the sex they identify with.

Sexuality

Sexuality is a way of talking about a person's sexual identity. This is to do with the ways in which a person may or may not feel attracted to people, and what people they are attracted to.

Gender Identity

Gender identity is a person's idea of how they are masculine, feminine, a mixture of both of these, or neither of them.

A Closer Look at the Letters

There are lots of different combinations and versions of LGBTQIA+ that people might use. As people learn more and more about sex, sexuality and gender, lots more letters and meanings can be added.

Bisexual
This is a person who is attracted to more than one gender.

Transgender
This is when a person's gender identity is different to the biological sex they were assigned at birth.

Gay
This can be men or women who are only attracted to people who are the same sex as them.

Lesbian
This is a woman who is only attracted to other women.

The LGBTQIA+ community is often represented by a rainbow flag. This is because it shows how everyone is different and unique and that it is these differences that are beautiful. Let's celebrate some members of the LGBTQIA+ community who have pride in themselves and their community, and have stood proud in the arts.

Queer
Someone might see themselves as queer if they feel their sexual and gender identities are anything other than heterosexual or cisgender.

Intersex
This is a person who is born with a mixture of sex characteristics that are seen as male and female, such as genitals and chromosomes.

Asexual
This is a person who does not feel sexually attracted to any sex or gender.

Plus
This is used to include all the letters that are missing from the abbreviation and to make sure everyone in the LGBTQIA+ community feels included regardless of who they are.

AUDRE LORDE

Born: 1934 Died: 1992

A Way with Words

Audre Lorde was born in New York City in the US. She started writing poetry at a very young age and had her first poem **published** at the age of 17. Throughout her life, she wrote many poems and essays about her experiences and thoughts as a Black lesbian woman.

Speaking Up and Speaking Out

She used her poetry as a way to speak up for the things she believed in. These problems were very similar to many other people's problems at the time, and her poetry gave these people a voice. She described herself as a 'Black, lesbian, mother, warrior poet'. She was also an **activist** who fought against **injustices** such as **racism**, **sexism**, **classism** and **homophobia**.

Sharing Is Caring

Lorde is remembered for fighting for many causes and not just ones that she experienced herself. She told people about the importance of sharing and talking about our experiences with others. She also taught us that by being ourselves, it can help people open up and support others.

> I learned so much from listening to people. And all I knew was, the only thing I had was honesty and openness.

WOMEN ARE POWERFUL & DANGEROUS

NO MORE VIOLENCE

GAY RIGHTS ARE HUMAN RIGHTS

LOVE

FIGHT BACK!

HAVE PRIDE

FREDDIE MERCURY

Born: 1946 Died: 1991

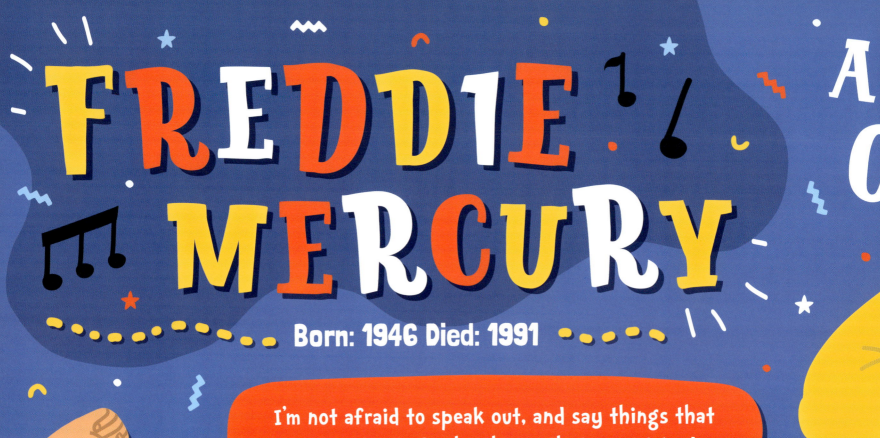

> I'm not afraid to speak out, and say things that I want to do, or do the things that I want to do... I think in the end, being natural, and being actually genuine is what wins.

A Person of Note

Freddie Mercury was born in Zanzibar in 1946. He was sent to school in India, where his parents were originally from. In 1964, Freddie and his family moved to England. Freddie was musical from a young age and began learning the piano at the age of seven.

From Minor to Major

Freddie was in lots of different bands throughout his life before taking over as the lead singer of a band that became Queen. Queen soared to fame in the 70s and 80s and to this day are seen as one of the most popular bands of all time.

Playing to His Own Beat

Freddie was always very flamboyant on stage and in the media. He was known for expressing both the feminine and masculine sides of his personality. He was also known for wearing clothes that were stereotypically seen as being either masculine or feminine. Although Freddie never said he was gay or bisexual, he was known to have relationships with both men and women.

Freddie's self-expression and sexuality reminds us that a person doesn't have to fit into any particular label or box, and you don't have to tell people about your identity if you don't want to.

RuPaul

Born: 1960

Paving the Runway

RuPaul was born in 1960 in California in the US. He moved around the US to perform on stage and screen, and found his fame in New York City. From a young age, RuPaul had always been interested in the performing arts and dressing up. This went on to shape his life as a popstar, TV show host, activist and, most importantly, drag queen. Now, he creates a platform for the LGBTQIA+ and drag communities across the world.

You're born naked and the rest is just drag.

What Is Drag?

Dressing in drag is when a person dresses up in a very exaggerated way that often includes playing on ideas of gender. For example, a person who sees themselves as a man might dress up in typically feminine clothes in order to perform. This is called being a drag queen. A person who sees themselves as a woman who dresses in typically masculine clothes is a drag king. Any gender can dress up in drag by performing in a way that exaggerates or plays with ideas of gender.

DRAGGING THE WORLD INTO THE FUTURE

RuPaul has been both a gay icon and a drag icon for many years. From small clubs to world-famous TV shows, he has helped make drag a respected and mainstream artform.

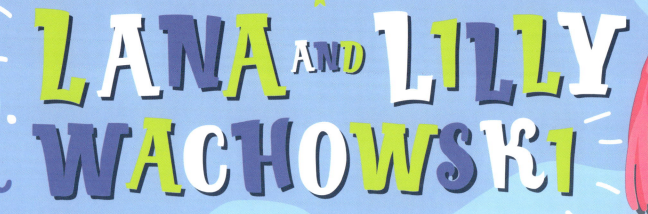

LANA AND LILLY WACHOWSKI

Lana Born: 1965 • Lilly Born: 1967

> There are some things we have to do for ourselves, but there are things that we do for other people.

LANA

And... Action!

Lilly and Lana Wachowski are film writers, producers, directors... and sisters! They are most well known for writing and creating *The Matrix* trilogy and many other blockbuster movies. Their films are full of action and make people think about life.

LILLY

Becoming Role Models

Lilly and Lana were both assigned male at birth, but later came out as transgender. Lana came out in 2012, and Lilly in 2016. In 2012, Lana won the Human Rights Campaign Visibility Award for representing transgender and LGBTQIA+ people. Lana said she remembers not seeing people of her gender identity in the media or in the film industry and this made her feel like she didn't know where her place was or what it looked like. In her acceptance speech for the award, she said that she hopes she can become this person for others.

What Is Coming Out?

Coming out is when a person chooses to tell someone about their sex, sexuality or gender identity. It is important to remember that a person doesn't have to come out unless they want to or are ready to. A person also doesn't have to come out to everyone they know at once — they can come out to whoever they want, whenever they want. It is their choice.

CHAZ BONO

Born: 1969

Changing to Chaz

Chaz Bono is the son of the US entertainers Sonny and Cher and, like his parents, he also went on to become a musician. Chaz was assigned female at birth, but later came out as gay and then transgender after the media began to guess what his sexuality was. Chaz underwent surgery to transition.

Telling His Story

After coming out and transitioning, Chaz became an activist for the LGBTQIA+ community. He has published books and made documentaries that explore his gender and sexuality and the story of his transition. He has used his voice to speak up for the LGBTQIA+ community and worked for charities such as GLAAD.

What Is Transitioning?

A transgender person may or may not choose to transition. Transitioning means a different thing to every person. It might involve medical transitioning, such as taking medication or having surgery. For someone else, it could involve telling friends and family, dressing differently and changing their name to one they feel suits them more.

BILLY PORTER

Born: 1969

Born to Perform

Billy Porter grew up in the US as a Black, gay, Christian man. Unfortunately, at this time, his religious community did not accept gay people and so, for much of his early life, Porter had to hide that part of himself from many of his friends and family. However, he had always known that he could entertain people from a young age.

Taking to the Stage...

Porter found a community that accepted him for who he was in the performing arts. After studying drama in his hometown of Pittsburgh, Pennsylvania, in the US, he moved to New York and went on to perform in the theatre, on TV and in film. He has won numerous awards for his roles which often explore gender fluidity. In 2019, he became the first openly gay Black man to win an **Emmy** for Lead Actor in a Drama Series.

We need to understand that whatever we do, we're always human beings first.

Strike a Pose

Porter is well known for his red carpet looks in which he often explores his gender by mixing masculine and feminine stereotypes in one outfit. Porter says that his time working on the TV series *Pose* helped him to understand more about his own gender identity and expression.

What Is Gender Fluidity and Gender Expression?

A person whose gender is fluid means that they might identify as either male or female at different times, or they might have multiple genders at once. It can also mean that a person's gender identity is constantly changing. Gender expression is how a person might choose to show their gender identity to the outside world through things such as their appearance, fashion choices and behaviour.

LENA WAITHE

Born: 1984

> The only way you really see change is by helping to create it.

Representing Her Community

Lena Waithe is a **screenwriter**, producer and actor from the US. She has become famous for her work in writing, creating and starring in TV shows and films that show Black LGBTQIA+ experiences. Waithe remembers not seeing people like her when watching TV with her family as a child and she hopes that by creating these shows and films, she is becoming a role model for other young, Black LGBTQIA+ people.

The things that make us different, those are our superpowers.

A Real-Life Superhero

Waithe has won many awards. The Trevor Project honoured her with the Hero Award in 2018 for advancing LGBTQIA+ representation on screen and in film and TV. She was also the first Black woman to be awarded with an Emmy for Outstanding Writing in a Comedy Series.

What Is LGBTQIA+ Representation on Screen?

LGBTQIA+ representation on screen is showing a range of people from the LGBTQIA+ community in films and TV shows playing many different types of roles. Representation allows people to see themselves in the media.

JANELLE MONÁE

Born: 1985

> Being a queer Black woman in America, I consider myself to be ... free ... I'm open to learning more about who I am.

All Over the Arts

Janelle Monáe is an American singer, songwriter and actor. She began her life in the arts on stage performing in musicals. From a young age, she wrote plays and songs herself and in later life she has gone on to release a number of albums and star in many award-winning films such as *Moonlight* and *Hidden Figures*.

Coming Out as Queer

Monáe kept her sexuality out of the media for a long time but then decided to discuss her identity. She explained that she has had relationships with both men and women and first thought she was bisexual. She then learned about pansexuality and realised that this fit with her sexual identity, too. She is 'a queer, Black woman' and talks about how she is ready to learn more about herself.

Be Open to Who You Are

Monáe's approach to her sexuality reminds us that we do not need to fully understand or label our sexuality or gender identity and that we can keep learning more about it as we grow and change.

What Is Pansexuality?

Pansexuality is when a person can be attracted to anyone regardless of their biological sex, sexuality, gender or gender identity.

You are only as beautiful as the many beautiful things you do for others.

KATE MOROSS

Born: 1986

To the Letter

Kate Moross is a British designer. From a young age, they were obsessed with drawing and lettering. Moross is also an illustrator and founder of their own **studio**, Studio Moross. Moross's work is very **rebellious** and they try to do new things with their designs. They have also worked as an art director on music videos, as well as on album artworks for artists such as Sam Smith.

I think people fall into different groups but don't necessarily have one category they identify as.

Coming Out as Non-Binary

Kate Moross told the world that they were **non-binary** on social media. Moross uses their platform to talk about the challenges that the LGBTQIA+ community face and what still needs to be done so that there is **equality** for all in the design world.

What's a Pronoun? He/She/They/Them

A person might choose to express their gender identity through the pronouns they use. A non-binary person might use they or them instead of he or she. This might be because they find it hard to identify with either he or she, or they don't agree that gender can be only male or female.

Kate Moross
(they/them)
Director

ROSIE JONES

Born: 1990

HA HA HA

Coming Up to The Mic

Rosie Jones is a British writer and comedian. She performs stand-up comedy shows and has appeared on and written for many TV shows. She is a gay woman who has ataxic cerebral palsy. She uses this to her advantage in her stand-up comedy and is always pushing the **boundaries** of what people find comfortable and challenging about disabled people, and turns this into comedy.

Finding the Line and Crossing It

Rosie is helping to change people's views and ideas of gay and disabled people by talking about how they can have LGBTQIA+ sexualities and gender identities in her comedy. She talks about how her comedy might make people uncomfortable at first, but that comedy allows people to understand more about LGBTQIA+ people who have disabilities.

What Is Ataxic Cerebral Palsy?

Cerebral palsy is when the brain becomes damaged and affects a person's movement. Ataxic cerebral palsy is a particular type of cerebral palsy that is caused by a brain injury that happens during or shortly after birth. It causes problems with movement and speech.

BE AN ALLY!

Even if you aren't a member of the LGBTQIA+ community, you can still support its members in being who they are and making sure they have equality. This is called being an ally. Here are a few ways you can be a good ally.

Listen

Always listen to people and learn about their lives and experiences. Listening can help us to understand the interesting differences between people.

Be an Influencer

Always be inclusive and invite LGBTQIA+ people to participate in the things you are doing. It is important to try to include different people from different backgrounds at all times.

Challenge and Report

If you see someone bullying anyone because of their sex, sexuality or gender identity, tell a grown-up that you trust straight away. If it is safe to do so, support the person that is being bullied by asking if they are okay and encourage them to tell a grown-up they trust about what happened.

Read Up and Ask Questions

It might seem a bit scary to talk to someone about their sex, sexuality or gender identity. It is important to read about the LGBTQIA+ community and ask people questions if you aren't sure of how to say something or talk to someone.

LAST BUT NOT LEAST

There are so many different and diverse people that have pride in who they are and in the arts. Here are some more people to look out for...

Amandla Stenberg
Stenberg is an actor who is gay.

Sam Smith
Smith is a singer and songwriter who is non-binary.

Lady Gaga
Gaga is a singer and songwriter who is bisexual.

Kim Petras
Petras is a singer and songwriter who is a transgender woman.

GLOSSARY

activist	a person who tries to make a change in the world by doing things such as going to marches
assigned	to be given without having a choice
attracted	to want to form a close, romantic or sexual relationship with someone
biological sex	whether a person's sex characteristics are considered to be male, female or intersex
biology	the science that studies the growth and life processes of living things
blockbuster	a film that cost a lot of money to make and has had a lot of success
boundaries	the edges or limits of something
chromosomes	tiny things inside cells (the building blocks that make up all living things) that give our bodies information about what to do and how to grow
cisgender	when a person's gender identity matches the biological sex they were assigned at birth
classism	the actions caused by the incorrect belief that some people from higher social classes are better than those from lower social classes
community	a group of people who are connected by something
directors	in film, people who are in charge of how the film will look and feel
Emmy	an award that recognises excellence in the writing and making of television shows
equality	the state of being equal, having the same opportunities and rights as someone else
feminine	things that are stereotypically associated with being female
flamboyant	to do something in an exaggerated or showy way
genitals	parts of the body between the legs
GLAAD	Gay & Lesbian Alliance Against Defamation, GLAAD is an organisation that makes sure the media covers LGBTQIA+ topics in the right way
heterosexual	only being attracted to people of the opposite sex to you
homophobia	an unjustified hatred or fear of gay people

icon	a very well-known or famous person who represents an idea of something
industry	all of the people and jobs that make up a particular area of work, for example the film industry
injustices	things that are not fair or right in the world
mainstream	to be known by most people in society
march	a large gathering of people who walk from one point to another in order to try to change or celebrate something
masculine	things that are stereotypicaly associated with being male
media	the different ways that information is shown to the public such as TV, adverts, newspapers and radio
non-binary	a person whose gender identity is not only male or female; non-binary can include people who have no gender, switch between genders or don't identify completely with any one gender
platform	the position a person holds that they can use to help make other people's voices and opinions heard
producers	people who help with the idea and creation of a piece of art such as a video or film
published	to have a piece of your work printed in something such as a book or magazine
racism	the actions caused by the incorrect belief that some people are better than others based on the way they look or where they come from
rebellious	doing things in a way that cannot be controlled
represented	acted as a symbol for something else
screenwriter	someone who writes the words for TV shows and films
sex characteristics	behaviours or physical features that tell you of a person's biological sex
sexism	the actions caused by the incorrect belief that some sexes are better than others
stereotypically	done in a way that uses beliefs which are not founded in facts but are believed by a lot of people
studio	an office or space where a group of people work
Trevor Project	an organisation that helps young LGBTQIA+ people

INDEX